D1738907

COPYRIGHT PAGE

Journeying Through Live

Copyright © 2023 by Danny Jones

Cover design by: Danny Jones

Printed in USA

Introduction:

Welcome to "Journeying Through Life," a devotional for everyday life. Life is a journey that we all embark upon, and it can be full of ups and downs, joys and sorrows, victories and defeats. Sometimes, it can be difficult to find the courage and inspiration we need to keep moving forward on our journey. That's where this devotional comes in.

"Journeying Through Life" is a collection of devotions that will help you find hope, encouragement, and inspiration for every day of your life. Each devotion is based on a different scripture and explores a unique theme, such as faith, love, gratitude, and forgiveness.

Whether you are facing a challenging season of life, or simply looking for a daily dose of spiritual inspiration, this devotional is for you. It is designed to help you connect with God, deepen your faith, and find the strength and courage you need to keep journeying through life.

So, join us on this journey and allow God to speak to your heart through these devotions. May they be a source of comfort, encouragement, and inspiration to you as you journey through life.

SHAKING OFF THE SNAKES

Acts 28:3-5 (NLT) "As Paul gathered an armful of sticks and was laying them on the fire, a poisonous snake, driven out by the heat, bit him on the hand. The people of the island saw it hanging from his hand and said to each other, "A murderer, no doubt! Though he escaped the sea, justice will not permit him to live." But Paul shook off the snake into the fire and was unharmed. The people waited for him to swell up or suddenly drop dead. But when they had waited a long time and saw that he wasn't harmed, they changed their minds and decided he was a god."

We are guilty of so many things according to the bible. If we think inappropriate thoughts, we have sinned, if we are angry with someone, we have sinned by murdering them in our hearts. As a result of this irrefutable law of nature, we can't be with God as is. However, because of what Jesus did, we are made right, whole and righteous.

The story of Paul and the poisonous snake has many lessons we can apply in our own lives. In this passage, we see Paul, bitten by a venomous snake while gathering sticks for a fire. The people around him assumed he was being punished for his past crimes and would soon die, they say he must be a murderer. However, Paul shook off the snake and was unharmed, leading the people to change their minds about him. The wild thing is, He was a murderer! Yet because of the forgiveness of the Lord and the new covenant that says we will not be harmed by snakes, Paul shook it off and was unharmed.

The first lesson we can learn is that sometimes the unexpected happens. Just like Paul was bitten by a snake when he was simply trying to gather firewood, we can be hit with unexpected challenges in our own lives. We must remember that just because we face unexpected obstacles doesn't mean that God is punishing us or that we are doomed to fail.

The second lesson we can take from this story is that we can shake off the things that try to harm us. Like Paul, we can choose to shake off the negative thoughts, doubts, and fears that try to take hold in our minds. We can trust in God's protection and know that we are not defined by our past mistakes.

Lastly, we see that the people around Paul changed their minds about him when they saw him survive the snakebite. This serves as a reminder that our actions can have a powerful impact on those around us. When we trust in God and overcome the obstacles in our lives, we can inspire others to do the same.

Remember, Paul was a murderer, worse than most of us, but God still said that he was redeemed. Let us embrace the unexpected, shake off the things that try to harm us, and inspire those around us with our actions. May we trust in God's protection and know that we are capable of overcoming any obstacle in our path.

In what way are you holding on to the old you?

Who is it that God says you are?

Prayer:

Dear Lord, we thank you for the lessons we can learn from the story of Paul and the poisonous snake. Help us to trust in your protection and to shake off the negative thoughts and doubts that try to hold us back. We pray that our actions inspire those around us and that we are able to overcome any obstacle in our path. In Jesus' name, we pray, Amen.

REVIVAL IS WAITING ON US

2 Chronicles 7:14 (NIV) - "if my people, who are called by my name, will humble themselves and pray and seek my face and turn from their wicked ways, then I will hear from heaven, and I will forgive their sin and will heal their land."

When I was starting out with my coaching company I had met with a high value potential client. I thought everything went well and so I created my proposal and sent it off to the client. Apparently I missed the email response from them, and being that I was early in my career, I was shy and felt like if I reached out, I would be too pushy. So I sent one response, and still didn't receive a response. After about a month or so I was going through old messages where I found the original response, then the response to the message I sent and then a final response that said they had decided to go with a different option because I didn't make a move.

I had been sitting sadly lamenting to the Lord while the whole time they were waiting on me! I just miscommunicated with them. I was so upset when I lost the contract. Revival can be the same way, many Christians today talk about the need for revival in our churches and communities. We long to see an outpouring of the Holy Spirit, a renewed passion for the things of God, and a turning away from sin. But what if I told you that revival is waiting for us? What if I said that God is ready and willing to move, but it's up to us to take the first step?

In 2 Chronicles 7:14, God gives us a clear roadmap for revival. He says that if His people will humble themselves, pray, seek His face, and turn from their wicked ways, then He will hear from heaven, forgive their sin, and heal their land. Notice that God doesn't say He will do these things unilaterally. He says that He will respond to our actions.

So what are we waiting for? Revival isn't some distant dream that we hope will one day come to us. It's a reality that is waiting for us to step into. We need to humble ourselves and acknowledge that we can't do it on our own. We need to pray and seek God's face, asking Him to move in our lives and in our communities. And we need to turn away from sin and pursue righteousness, so that we can be vessels of revival in a dark and broken world.

Revival isn't waiting on us. It's waiting for us. God is ready to move, but He needs willing hearts and surrendered lives. Let's be the people who prepare the way for revival in our churches, our communities, and our world.

What can you do to focus on purifying your life to prepare for revival?

Prayer:

Heavenly Father, we come before you today with humble hearts and open hands. We acknowledge that we need revival in our lives and in our communities. We ask that you would help us to be the people who prepare the way for your Spirit to move. Help us to pray, seek your face, and turn from our wicked ways. We believe that you are ready and willing to move, and we ask that you would use us as vessels of your love and power. In Jesus' name we pray, Amen.

TRUSTING THE PROCESS SO WE CAN BE TRUSTED WITH THE PROMISE

"Let us not become weary in doing good, for at the proper time we will reap a harvest if we do not give up."- Galatians 6:9 (NIV)

I once heard a story of a man who was the foreman of a decently profitable construction company. His boss promised that when things were going well enough, as a bonus he would get a house. Excitedly he waited for the boss to say the time was right. After a couple of years he began to grow impatient. Then one day the boss had a meeting with him to discuss a new upcoming project. The boss starts out by saying he is very grateful for the performance of the team under the foreman's leadership. He says the time for him to be able to have his house will be soon.

The boss then explains that this next project is going to be special, the company is going to be building a new house for the boss himself. He says to the foreman, because this house is for me and my family, I want you to take extra care in the building process and material. He also says if you need to spend extra money to make sure it's the best, go for it.

Filled with frustration and bitterness because he felt like he's never going to get his house and now this happened; The foreman decided to do the opposite of the request. Out of spite, he built the project with cheaper material, and cut a lot of corners. He allowed the workers to take off early in order to give the appearance that they were spending all the time they needed to create a quality home.

When he completed the project the boss came to inspect. The boss asked the foreman if the home was built to specifications. He repeated to him, it was really important that his family had the best. The foreman said, "Of course." The boss responded, "I am really happy to hear that." As he finished talking with his foreman he pulled out a folder. Inside was the deed to the home with the foreman's name on it. The boss says, "I am so grateful for all the work you have done for me. I consider you family so I wanted to wait until we were doing well enough that I could afford to build you a house that you deserve. One that could adequately measure up to all that you have meant to me and this company."

Life can be full of uncertainties, and it's easy to become impatient and anxious when we're waiting for something to happen. But as believers, we know that God has a plan for our lives, and that everything that happens to us is part of His divine process. When we learn to trust in the process, we can be confident that God will fulfill His promises to us. If we are going to be trusted with the process - growing a ministry, gaining financially, seeing others healed, whatever it is that God has placed in your heart, you need to be willing to trust the process.

Trusting in the process means that we believe that God is working behind the scenes, even when we can't see what He's doing. We may not know when or how God will answer our prayers, but we can trust that He is faithful and that His timing is perfect.

The Bible is full of stories of people who had to trust in the process. Abraham waited for years for God to fulfill His promise to give him a son, and Joseph had to endure many trials and setbacks before he became second in command in Egypt. But both of these men trusted in God, and in the end, they saw His faithfulness.

If we want to be trusted with God's promises, we need to learn to trust in the process. It's so easy to be seduced by the desire to get things done quickly. Most things that are worth anything take time. It is never easy to wait, but it worth it.

What is something that you have been waiting for?

What are you going to do in the waiting to continue to be ready and to make sure that you don't start to cut corners out of impatience?

Prayer:

Dear God, thank You for Your faithfulness and Your perfect timing. Help us to trust in the process, and to surrender our plans and our timelines to You. Give us faith to believe that You are working behind the scenes, and that Your promises for us will come to pass in Your perfect timing. We trust You, Lord, and we know that You are always faithful. In Jesus' name, Amen!

PUTTING YOUR OXYGEN MASK ON FIRST

"Love your neighbor as yourself." - Matthew 22:39 (NIV)

Have you ever been on an airplane and listened to the safety instructions? One of the things that I am sure you have heard is that in the event of an emergency, you secure your own oxygen mask before you . This may seem counterintuitive, but it's actually crucial. If we don't take care of ourselves first, we won't be able to help anyone else.

The same principle applies to our daily lives. What if in everything we did, we put our oxygen mask on first? What if we prioritized our own healing and wholeness, so that we could be better equipped to love and serve those around us?

When we take care of ourselves, we become healthier, stronger, and more resilient. We become better equipped to handle the challenges of life, and to love and serve others with joy and grace. When we prioritize our own healing and wholeness, we become better neighbors, friends, spouses, parents, and coworkers.

But how do we prioritize our own healing and wholeness? The first step is to recognize that we are valuable and worthy of love and care. God created us in His image, and He loves us deeply. We need to prioritize our relationship with Him, spending time in prayer, reading His Word, and worshiping Him. When we are connected to God, we are filled with His love and His strength.
We also need to take care of our physical, emotional, and mental health. This may mean taking time for exercise, eating healthy foods, getting enough sleep, and seeking professional help when needed. It may mean setting healthy boundaries with toxic people or situations, and surrounding ourselves with positive influences.

When we prioritize our own healing and wholeness, we become better equipped to love and serve others. We become more patient, compassionate, and understanding. We become better listeners, and more empathetic. We become more like Jesus, who loved and served others with humility and grace. Furthermore, would you want to be treated by someone else, the way you treat yourself? The scripture says, we are to love others the way we lover ourselves.

So today, let's put on our oxygen mask first. Let's prioritize our own healing and wholeness, so that we can love and serve those around us with joy and grace. Let's remember that we are valuable and worthy of love and care, and let's seek God's strength and guidance in all that we do.

What are some of the areas that you are neglecting your own health or longevity?

What can you do to begin to change in order to make sure you will be able to continue the race?

Prayer:

Dear God, thank You for loving us and creating us in Your image. Help us to prioritize our own healing and wholeness, so that we can love and serve those around us with joy and grace. Fill us with Your strength and Your love, and help us to seek You in all that we do. May we become more like Jesus, who loved and served others with humility and grace. In His name we pray, Amen.

WE ALL NEED SOMEBODYTO LEAN ON

"The way of a fool is right in his own eyes, but a wise man listens to advice." - Proverbs 12:15 (NIV)

When I was around 10 years old, I decided that I wanted to build a hang glider. Given that I obviously didn't have any aeronautical engineering knowledge and this was long before the days of the internet, I built it based on what I remembered seeing in movies or pictures. So I got out our saw and I started cutting up some wooden 2x4s so I could make the frame of the aircraft. Then I got some trash bags to make the sail. Once it was stapled on, I started climbing a ladder to test it out.

Thankfully as I climbed the ladder my dad rounded the corner to the backyard. He had brought my mom and they were able to kindly make me pause. They told me that when you build something that carries people you always test it with something that can't hurt so you can make adjustments then fly in it as a person. Obviously since there was nothing about this that would fly; It fell straight to the ground after I tied my blanket and some things to it and threw it from the ladder.

In today's world, many people are learning online. Whether it's a new skill, a hobby, or even a college degree, the internet has made it possible for us to learn from anywhere in the world. While online learning has many benefits, there's one thing that it can't replace: the guidance of a mentor or teacher. The value of having someone who has already been there, or has a little more life experience than you do is invaluable.

Think about it: when you're learning to sing or exercise, you need someone to watch you and give you feedback. You need someone to tell you if you're doing something wrong, and to help you adjust your technique so that you don't get hurt. The same is true in other areas of life. Whether it's a career, a relationship, or even our spiritual life, we need someone who can guide us and give us wise advice.

In the Bible, we see many examples of people who had mentors. David had Samuel, Elijah had Elisha, and Jesus had

His disciples. These mentors helped their students grow and develop, both spiritually and in other areas of their lives. They provided guidance, wisdom, and support, helping their students to become the best versions of themselves.

As Christians, we are called to be mentors to one another. We are called to love and serve one another, and to help each other grow in our faith. But we are also called to seek out mentors for ourselves. We need people who can guide us, teach us, and hold us accountable.

If you're learning something new online, consider finding a mentor who can help you along the way. Look for someone who is knowledgeable and experienced in your field, and who shares your values and goals. Pray for God's guidance and wisdom as you search for a mentor, and be open to the guidance of the Holy Spirit.

Remember, the way of a fool is right in his own eyes, but a wise person listens to advice. Don't be afraid to seek out a mentor or teacher who can help you grow and develop. And don't forget to be a mentor to others, sharing your knowledge and wisdom with those who are just starting out.

Who in your life, reflects Jesus the way you would like to?

Be brave and go and offer to buy them a coffee and let them know you are looking for a mentor. If you already have one, take this reminder to thank them for what they have done in your life.

Prayer:

Dear God, thank You for the many blessings that You have given us, including the ability to learn new things. Help us to seek out mentors who can guide us and help us grow in our faith and in other areas of our lives. Give us wisdom as we choose mentors, and help us to be open to the guidance of the Holy Spirit. And help us to be mentors to others, sharing our knowledge and wisdom with those who are just starting out. In Jesus' name we pray, Amen.

OVERCOMING DOUBT

""But he must ask in faith without any doubting, for the one who doubts is like the surf of the sea, driven and tossed by the wind."." - James 1:6 (NASB)

When I was around the second grade, a man I had met who was a successful veterinarian showed up on Christmas morning and had a gift for all five of us children. See, my parents were artist and not financially well off. This man brought gifts for all of my four older siblings and then said he couldn't figure out how to wrap my gift and he needed help getting it out of the car. He had previously asked me questions about my bicycle that had no tires, and I thought it was just normal conversation, little did I know what he was really planning. I had wanted a new bicycle that would be safer and more fun to ride for over a year, (that's a really long time in the second and third grade). My father had promised if he sold a specific bowl at the gallery he would buy me a bicycle but at this point, it had been over sitting in the gallery for a few years already with little interest. I had just accepted the fact that I would never get a new bicycle.

We all went out to his car where he opened his trunk and I could see his bicycle tire. He pulled it out so we could get to my gift, but he didn't move anymore after he pulled out his bike. He was standing there with a smile and I was unclear about what was happening, until he said, "This is for you." I was so confused, I knew what he was saying, but my brain couldn't comprehend. I had fully accepted the fact that my parents wouldn't be able to afford a bicycle I asked him if he was sure it was mine and not a mistake multiple times.

In the book of Luke, we read about a man named Zachariah who was visited by an angel. The angel told him that his wife Elizabeth would give birth to a son, who would be a great prophet of God. Zachariah was surprised and skeptical, and he asked the angel how he could be sure that this would happen.

On one hand, it's easy to understand why Zachariah would be doubtful. He and his wife were old and had never been able to have children. The idea that they would suddenly have a child in their old age was hard to believe. But his doubt also reveals a deeper issue: a lack of faith. On the other hand,

How broken does a person need to be to not believe what a 10 foot angel says to you?

Like Zachariah, we all experience doubt at times. We question whether God is really listening to our prayers, whether He cares about our struggles, and whether His promises are really true. And when we're in the midst of doubt, it can be hard to see a way out.

But the Bible tells us that doubt is not a sign of weakness or failure. It's a natural part of our human experience. The key is not to let doubt overcome us. Instead, we must learn to overcome doubt with faith.

James 1:6 says that when we ask God for something, we must believe and not doubt. When we doubt, we are like a wave of the sea, blown and tossed by the wind. But when we have faith, we are anchored in the truth of God's promises. We can weather any storm that comes our way, knowing that God is with us and that His promises are true.

If you're struggling with doubt today, take heart. You're not alone. But don't let doubt consume you. Instead, turn to God in prayer, and ask Him to help you overcome your doubts. Spend time reading His Word and meditating on His promises. And seek out the support of other believers who can encourage you in your faith.

Remember, Zachariah's doubt didn't prevent God from fulfilling His promise. In the same way, your doubts don't have to hold you back. Trust in God's goodness, and have faith that He will fulfill His promises in your life.

What are some areas that you are doubting the Lord?

Why are you doubting? Have you seen Him move similarly before?

If not, start asking those around you if they have any stories of when the Lord moved when they needed a miracle.

Prayer:

Dear God, I confess that I struggle with doubt at times. I question whether You are really listening to my prayers, and whether Your promises are really true. But I know that You are faithful, and that You will never leave me or forsake me. Help me to overcome my doubts with faith, and to trust in Your goodness and love. Give me the courage to seek out the support of other believers, and to turn to You in prayer and meditation. In Jesus' name I pray, Amen.

CORRECTING WITH LOVE

"Preach the word; be ready in season and out of season; reprove, rebuke, and exhort, with complete patience and teaching."- 2 Timothy 4:2 (ESV)

When I was a young believer, I was met with so much grace that I more or less never wanted to offend anyone. I was so grateful for the mess that God had pulled me out of that I never even wanted to raise my voice at someone. A few years back a friend of 15 or so years tells me that he is going to pick up one of those vape pens. I was really concerned because, I can still struggle with feeling like I am getting in people's way from happiness when I correct them. I carefully mentioned about some of the concerning data about the dangers of Vaping. He, being a smart and reasonable man looked into it and decided not to pursue the idea further.

At first, I felt bad about confronting him. Then I realized how crazy that sounded when I said it to myself. How could I stand by and not share with one of my best mates that he was about to walk into something that to the best of my knowledge was very dangerous How often do we do this on perhaps smaller things, maybe bigger things like sin and salvation.

As followers of Christ, we are called to preach the Word and to correct, rebuke, and encourage others. But as the prompt acknowledges, it can be difficult to find the balance between correction and harsh rebuke. We may fear that our words will be too strong, or that we will hurt someone's feelings.

But the Bible tells us that correction is an act of love. Hebrews 12:6 says, "The Lord disciplines the one he loves, and he chastens everyone he accepts as his son." When we correct someone, we are showing them that we care about them and want them to grow in their faith.

At the same time, we must be careful to correct with love and compassion. Ephesians 4:15 tells us to "speak the truth in love." This means that we should always approach correction with a spirit of gentleness and humility. We should seek to build up, rather than tear down.

2 Timothy 4:2 reminds us to be prepared to correct, rebuke, and encourage "with great patience and careful instruction."

This means that we should take the time to carefully consider our words, and to approach correction with a spirit of patience and understanding. We should be willing to listen to the other person's perspective, and to work together to find a solution.

But even as we strive to correct with love, we may still struggle with our own weaknesses and shortcomings. As the prompt acknowledges, we may feel overwhelmed by the pain and brokenness we see in the world around us. We may struggle with our own sins and failings.

In those moments, we can turn to God for strength and guidance. We can pray for His help in overcoming our weaknesses and becoming more like Him. And we can trust in His promise to make us whole and restore us to His image.

Let us strive to correct, rebuke, and encourage others with love and patience, trusting in God's strength and guidance each step of the way.

What are some ways that you have held back in areas that you really need to speak up?

How can you deliver correction from a place of love that is encouraging and helps someone grow?

Prayer:

Dear God, thank you for calling us to preach the Word and to correct, rebuke, and encourage others. Help us to approach this task with love, patience, and compassion, always seeking to build up rather than tear down. Give us the wisdom to know when to correct and when to be patient, and the courage to speak the truth in love. And help us to trust in Your strength and guidance as we seek to become more like You each day. In Jesus' name we pray, Amen.

THE DIRECTION OF OUR EYES

Psalm 121:1-2,(NASB) "I will lift up my eyes to the mountains; From where shall my help come? My help comes from the Lord, Who made heaven and earth."

I love to ride motorcycles. There are not many picturesque places like my home in Hawaii. I took the motorcycle safety course when I first wanted to ride because I thought that would be the smartest thing to do. One of the first things they talked about was what to do while turning. It was always "Look where you are turning" So if you are going to turn right, you don't look forward as you turn, you look to the right and pick the point that you are going to end up at.

As humans, we have a tendency to focus on what's in front of us, what we can see with our physical eyes. But sometimes, what we see in front of us can be overwhelming and discouraging. It's during these times that we need to lift our eyes up and focus on something greater than ourselves. As the psalmist writes, "I lift up my eyes to the mountains— where does my help come from? My help comes from the Lord, the Maker of heaven and earth."

Just as looking where we want to turn on a motorcycle helps us stay on course, looking to the Lord helps us stay on the right path. When we focus our attention on the Lord, we are reminded of His sovereignty and goodness. We are reminded that He is in control and that He has a plan for our lives. It's easy to get bogged down by the problems and challenges we face, but when we keep our eyes on the Lord, we are able to persevere and overcome.

But what does it mean to keep our eyes on the Lord? It means seeking Him through prayer, reading His Word, and worship. It means trusting in His promises and seeking His will for our lives. It means recognizing that we are not in control, but that He is. When we keep our eyes on the Lord, we are able to see beyond our current circumstances and trust in His plan for our lives.

However, just like with a motorcycle, it's easy to get distracted and take our eyes off the road. Life can throw us curveballs and we can become overwhelmed by our circumstances. It's during these times that we need to intentionally refocus our attention on the Lord. We need to remind ourselves of His goodness and faithfulness. We need to trust in His plan and His timing.

As we journey through life, remember to fix your eyes on the Lord, his call and purpose. Let's trust in His plan and seek His will for our lives. Let's not be discouraged by the challenges and obstacles we face, but instead, let's lift our eyes up to the mountains and remember that our help comes from the Lord, the Maker of heaven and earth.

What have you been looking at recently?

What is something that you do that helps to refocus your attention on the Lord?

Prayer

Heavenly Father, help us to keep our eyes fixed on You. In the midst of the challenges and difficulties we face, help us to trust in Your plan and Your timing. Give us the strength and courage to persevere and overcome. Thank You for Your goodness and faithfulness. In Jesus' name, Amen.

BEING GRATEFUL
WHEN IT'S HARD

1 Thessalonians 5:16-18, (NIV)
"Rejoice always, pray continually, give
thanks in all circumstances; for this is
God's will for you in Christ Jesus."

There was a period of time where things went badly. I have experienced a great number of hardships in my life as everyone does but this particular season was a little bit much for me. The end of a year, my cousin passed away, the beginning of the following year, I found my mother on the floor after having fallen and lying there for around 24 hours. My company was not doing well so financially I was really falling into a hole. Toward the third quarter of the year, I found my father on the floor in his apartment after about 14 hours, delirious and not well. While he was in the hospital he had another heart attack. Shortly after my Aunt passed away. Around Christmas time, we almost lost my sister due to some health complications.

At the behest of my counselor, I was told to take my first ever vacation. Even though finances were tight, I knew I needed some space to try to clear my head and get a break from all that I was facing; an opportunity to refocus on God's plan for my life. Since I already had a credit for the airline and, friends I could stay with I decided to go to a wedding in Europe for a dear friend, I decided to go for it. I had two projects lined up the month and a half before my flight which both fell through. I wanted to cancel my trip but I knew I really needed to get some space to find out the direction the Lord wanted me to go.

While I was on vacation, I stopped off in Italy to scout out something for a ministry opportunity. The morning I was going to go survey the land, I woke up to a text that my sister did indeed pass away. I was crushed, I was completely alone (which is something that more or less never happens being from an island) It was the one day that I would spend the entire day away from any of my friends. I shortened my trip and flew home. About a week after I got home, my dad shares he has cancer.

I decide to look for a job since my company was struggling so badly. One day around 100 applications in sitting at a coffee shop I love, I ran into the parents of one of my former students. They informed me that their daughter had died suddenly.

1 Thessalonians 5:18 is, in my opinion one of the more misinterpreted scriptures. Unfortunately when you change one single word it transforms the entire meaning. I have heard sermons and quotes that say "For" not "In". There is a completely different meaning when you are being told by the manual of life, "Be thankful FOR all circumstances." As opposed to, "Be thankful IN all circumstances."

I am a reasonably smart guy but there is no way I can spin these circumstances to say, Thank you Lord that my sister died, and that I am struggling financially, and my parents are getting older etc… However, I am able to give thanks to the Lord that I am still breathing, and that He is still on the throne. Sometimes, all we can thank the Lord for is the breath in our lungs. This is a skill that we have to train and exercise regularly to be better.

In our lives, we often find ourselves complaining about the things that we don't have or the things that we wish were different. It's easy to get caught up in negativity and forget to appreciate the good things that we have. But when we cultivate an attitude of gratitude, our whole perspective changes.

Gratitude is a powerful force that can transform our lives. When we choose to give thanks in all circumstances, we begin to see the good in everything. We start to focus on the blessings that we have rather than the things that we lack. We become more content and less focused on what we don't have.

When we rejoice always and pray continually, we invite God's presence into our lives. We acknowledge that He is in control and that He has a plan for us. We trust that even in the difficult times, He is working all things together for our good.

Giving thanks in all circumstances isn't always easy. Sometimes life throws us curveballs that make it hard to see the good. But even in those moments, we can choose to focus on the blessings that we do have. We can give thanks for the people in our lives who love and support us. We can give thanks for the roof over our heads and the food on our tables. We can give thanks for the breath in our lungs and the beating of our hearts.

So let us cultivate an attitude of gratitude. Let us give thanks in all circumstances and rejoice always. As we do, we will find that our hearts are filled with joy and our minds are at peace. For this is God's will for us in Christ Jesus.

What are three things that you could be thankful for right now?

Find someone to share these three things with so it can become a deeper part of your life.

Prayer:

Heavenly Father, thank you for the many blessings in my life. Help me to cultivate an attitude of gratitude and to give thanks in all circumstances. May my heart be filled with joy and my mind at peace as I trust in You. In Jesus' name, Amen

KEEP YOUR EYES ON THE PRIZE

Philippians 3:14 (NIV) - "I press on toward the goal to win the prize for which God has called me heavenward in Christ Jesus."

When we throw a dart or shoot an arrow, we don't look at all the things we don't want to hit. We don't focus on the negative outcomes or the obstacles in our way. Instead, we keep our eyes on the target and aim for the bullseye.

In a coaching session, I was coaching a client once and they said "I can't believe I did this. I have become my father. I swore I would never be like him." This was a prime example of focusing on what you don't want and hitting it as a target instead.

In life, it's easy to get caught up in the distractions and negativity that surrounds us. We can become so focused on what's wrong that we forget to look for what's right. However, as Christians, we are called to a higher purpose and to strive for the goals that God has set for us. In this devotional, we will explore the importance of keeping our eyes on the prize and following the path that God has set for us.

As Christians, we are called to a life of purpose and fulfillment. God has given us unique talents, abilities, and passions that can be used to glorify Him and make a positive impact in the world. However, to achieve these goals, we need to keep our eyes on the prize and focus on the end result. This means setting goals that align with God's will and actively working towards them with faith and perseverance.

Keeping our eyes on the prize doesn't mean that we will never face obstacles or challenges. In fact, it's often through these struggles that we grow and develop into the person that God has called us to be. However, when we keep our eyes fixed on the end goal, we can overcome these obstacles with determination and faith. We can trust that God has a plan for our lives and that He will guide us through any difficulties we may face.

In order to keep our eyes on the prize, we need to take practical steps towards our goals. This means creating a plan, breaking down our goals into smaller steps, and being disciplined in our daily habits. We also need to surround ourselves with positive influences, such as other Christians who can encourage us and hold us accountable.

As we go about our daily lives, let us remember to keep our eyes on the prize and focus on the goals that God has set for us. Let us have faith that He will guide us through any obstacles or challenges that we may face, and trust that His plan for our lives is greater than anything we could ever imagine. With God's help, we can hit the bullseye of our aspirations and live a life of purpose and fulfillment.

What are some positive things you can start focusing on right now?

What are things you can speak life into right now to begin to change your focus?

Prayer:
Dear God, we thank You for the unique gifts and abilities that You have given us. Help us to focus on the goals that You have set for us and to trust in Your plan for our lives. Give us the strength and perseverance to overcome any obstacles that we may face, and surround us with positive influences that will encourage and support us. May we glorify You in all that we do and live a life of purpose and fulfillment. In Jesus' name, we pray, Amen.

THE POWER OF ONE

John 6:8-9 (NIV) - "Another of his disciples, Andrew, Simon Peter's brother, spoke up, "Here is a boy with five small barley loaves and two small fish, but how far will they go among so many?"

When I was little, my dad would take me to the florist to buy my mom flowers. I didn't have any money but I would get to pick them out and give them to my mom and say, "Mom I bought these for you." That's true, but it's also not accurate. My dad would provide the money and the ride to get there because at 5 years old, there was no possible way for me to buy flowers for my mom. Due to the generosity of my dad, I got to participate in being a blessing to my mom

Everything that I have, every skill, strength, talent, all of my finances, are because of the Lord. When He asks me to preach, regardless of how I feel, I preach. When He asks me to give, I give, when He tells me to go, I go. I would be lying if I said, I bat 1000 or that I don't argue with the Lord at first, probably the majority of the time. But, since I know that the Lord has given me the gift to do something, I will use it for His glory when He asks me.

The story of Jesus feeding the 5000 is one of the most well-known miracles in the Bible. But beyond the miracle itself, there is a powerful lesson that we can learn from the little boy who brought the only food he had. While many may have been too ashamed or too afraid to offer what little they had, this boy stepped forward and gave what he could.

The truth is that often, we may feel like our contributions are insignificant. We may think that our small acts of kindness or our limited resources won't make much of a difference in the grand scheme of things. But the story of the feeding of the 5000 reminds us that our faithfulness and willingness are what count. The small things that we do can have a big impact when we offer them with a spirit of generosity and faith.

Like the little boy who gave his lunch to Jesus, we too can offer what we have to the Lord and trust that He will use it to accomplish His purposes. Whether it's offering our time to serve others, giving what little we can to support a worthy cause, or simply being kind to those around us, every act of love and service can make a difference in someone's life.

Is there something that you have been hiding or holding back from the Lord?

If a little boy can offer his lunch and be recorded in the bible for his great gift, how much more can you give to see people blessed?

Prayer:

Dear Lord, help us to have the faith and courage to offer what we have to You, even if it seems small and insignificant. Use our gifts and talents to make a difference in the world and to bring glory to Your name. Help us to remember that every little bit counts, and that even the smallest acts of love and kindness can have a big impact. In Jesus' name, we pray. Amen.

TRUSTING IN GOD'S REVELATION

John 15:5 (ESV) - "I am the vine; you are the branches. Whoever abides in me and I in him, he it is that bears much fruit, for apart from me you can do nothing."

Very early in my professional life, I was working at a typical dead end job where the management wasn't all that concerned about what happened in the restaurant. There was a season of time where we were basically unsupervised. None of us chose call the main management to ask our questions or to report the lack of supervision. We just kept going and began to make up all our own rules, it was the lord of the flies, restaurant version. Sure enough things started to fall apart and the restaurant ended up closing.

It was a similar situation for the children of Israel. For the 400 years before Jesus' arrival, there was silence from heaven. They had no fresh revelation from God and had to rely on their own interpretation of the scriptures. When Jesus came, they didn't recognize him as the Son of God because they were relying on their own understanding instead of seeking a relationship with God.

In our own lives, we can fall into the same trap. When we don't seek God and get our information from him, we start to make things up for ourselves and create our own interpretation of what God wants. We rely on our own understanding instead of trusting in God's revelation.

Trusting in God means surrendering our own understanding and submitting to His will. It means seeking Him in prayer and studying His Word. When we trust in God's revelation, we can experience His guidance and wisdom in our lives. We can have confidence in His plan for us and trust that He will make our paths straight.

But it's not always easy to trust in God's revelation. We may face doubt or uncertainty about the path ahead. We may question if we are truly hearing from God. In those moments, we need to remember to lean not on our own understanding, but to submit to God and trust in His plan for our lives.

Thankfully we have the holy spirit and the veil blocking us from the Lord is gone. This means that there can't be a time for us where God is silent, only a time where we aren't hearing. He may not be speaking but he is not away from us as it was before Jesus' arrival.

When is the last time you sat down and were quiet with the Lord?

Prayer:
Dear God, help us to trust in your revelation and not lean on our own understanding. Give us the courage to submit to your will and seek you in all things. May we have confidence in your plan for our lives and trust that you will make our paths straight. We pray that we will not create our own interpretation of what you want but rely on your wisdom and guidance. In Jesus' name we pray, Amen.

BEING YOUR OWN ALLY

Psalm 139:13-14 (NIV) - "For you created my inmost being; you knit me together in my mother's womb. I praise you because I am fearfully and wonderfully made; your works are wonderful, I know that full well."

I was working with a coaching client once and they were sharing story after story of problems that they had encountered. At some point, I noticed a very interesting trend. I asked her if she noticed a common denominator in all the situations she shared. After some thought she did exclaimed with a laugh, "Me! It's me! I'm the common denominator." We discussed it further and she realized that although much of what happened wasn't her fault, she definitely put herself in situations that added to her problems.

After that coaching session, I began to reflect on my own life and the lives of all people. We are truly the only person who is with us every moment from our birth until our death. It's not uncommon to hear people talk about being their own worst enemy. We often criticize ourselves, hold ourselves to impossible standards, and allow negative self-talk to dominate our inner dialogue. But what if we chose to be our own ally instead? What if we chose to be with ourselves and for ourselves, right or wrong, ride or die?

We are the only ones who truly know ourselves, our thoughts, our feelings, and our experiences. And yet, we can be quick to turn against ourselves when things don't go as planned or we make mistakes.

But what if we took a cue from Psalm 139:13-14 and recognized that we are fearfully and wonderfully made? What if we embraced our strengths, our unique qualities, and the things that make us who we are? What if we were kind to ourselves and spoke to ourselves the way we would speak to a beloved friend?

Choosing to be your own ally doesn't mean you have to be perfect or never make mistakes. It means you recognize your inherent worth and value, and you choose to support yourself through the ups and downs of life. It means you believe in yourself and your abilities, and you refuse to let negative self-talk hold you back.

It's important to note that being your own ally doesn't mean you go it alone. We all need support from others, whether it's a friend, family member, pastor, or mental health professional. But when you choose to be your own ally, you open yourself up to a world of possibilities and opportunities. You become your own advocate, your own cheerleader, and your own source of strength and encouragement.

So the next time you feel yourself turning against yourself, remember that you are fearfully and wonderfully made. Choose to be your own ally and believe in yourself, even when it feels like no one else does. With God's help, you can be the best ally you've ever had.

What lies have you been believing and speaking over your life?

What are the truths that you can begin to speak over your life that the Father already knows about you?

Prayer:

Dear God, thank you for creating me fearfully and wonderfully. Help me to recognize my worth and value, and to be my own ally through the ups and downs of life. Give me the strength to support myself and believe in myself, even when things get tough. And help me to remember that with you by my side, I can do all things. Amen.

I AM WORTHY BECAUSE HE PAID THE PRICE

"But God demonstrates his own love for us in this: While we were still sinners, Christ died for us." - Romans 5:8 (NIV)

Art is a very funny and subjective world. Something that I may think is a worthless pile of trash someone else may pay thousands or more for. Van Gogh's work was worthless in his lifetime, but is now among the most expensive paintings in existence. But why? What changes the value of something. It is as simple as this, ask any great business person, something is worth what something will pay for it.

Do you ever struggle with feeling unworthy or undeserving of love and grace? Perhaps you have made mistakes or experienced failures in your life that make you feel like you don't deserve forgiveness or second chances. But the truth is, your worth is not based on your past or your performance. Your worth is based on what Jesus was willing to pay for you.

Romans 5:8 reminds us that while we were still sinners, Christ died for us. He didn't wait for us to clean up our act or earn His love. He loved us first and paid the ultimate price for our salvation. If Jesus was willing to give His life for us, how can we say that we are not worthy?

When we believe that we are unworthy or unlovable, we are essentially saying that the price Jesus paid was not enough. We are saying that His sacrifice on the cross was not sufficient to cover our sins and make us right with God. But the truth is, Jesus paid the price in full. He said, "It is finished" (John 19:30) as He breathed His last breath on the cross. He paid the price for our sins so that we could be reconciled to God and have eternal life.

So if Jesus decided that you were worth such a great cost, who are you to say that you are worthless? Your value is not based on your past, your mistakes, or your performance. Your value is based on what Jesus was willing to pay for you. You are loved, cherished, and valued by the God of the universe.

Today, let us remember that our worth is not based on our own merit, but on the price Jesus paid for us on the cross. Let us embrace our value and worth as children of God, and live in the freedom that comes from knowing we are loved and accepted just as we are.

What is your current belief about your worth?

Spend some time and ask the Lord, what He thinks your worth.

Prayer:

Heavenly Father, thank You for loving us so much that You sent Your Son to die for us on the cross. Help us to see our true value and worth as children of God, and to live in the freedom that comes from knowing we are loved and accepted by You. Help us to embrace the truth that we are worthy because of what Jesus has done for us, and to live each day with confidence and hope. In Jesus' name we pray, amen.

THE HUMAN EXPERIENCE: IT'S OKAY TO BE HURTING

2 Corinthians 1:3-4 (NIV)- "Blessed be the God and Father of our Lord Jesus Christ, the Father of mercies and God of all comfort, who comforts us in all our affliction, so that we may be able to comfort those who are in any affliction, with the comfort with which we ourselves are comforted by God."

Hurt is a strange thing. We inherently don't want to feel the pain, because well, it hurts. But pain is how our brain understands something is wrong.

I was quietly enjoying my coffee one day and a woman came up to me and asked if I could pray for her. She shared that she has been struggling with focus in her work recently. I asked her how long she's been doing her current job. She said for more than 20 years. The more we talked the more I could tell there was something deeper that was going on. Finally I asked her when did all this start, she said that it was about 6 months prior. I then pressed on to ask if there was anything significant that happened at that time.

Apparently a child who she was a caregiver for, passed due to an accident on her day off. When I asked her how she was feeling about it, she said she is fine because Jesus healed her. As we spoke, I felt as though maybe she was not being honest about how she was feeling. So I asked her a few more times how she was feeling about the loss and she gave in. She began to retell how broken her heart was. She also shared how she felt worse because she knew that as a believer God can heal her, and so she is supposed to be healed by already.

I shared that there is nothing wrong with being hurt and sad, and that God and does heal, but sometimes we have to walk through the process of healing. In the end I told her that she needed a small group that she could share with every week the truth, if she is having a good day/week, she needs to share it. If she is having a bad day/week she needs to share that too. She needs to have a group that will have the capacity to hear how she is actually doing every week until she is truly feeling okay.

I checked in with her a few years later and she shared, "Honestly, the following year or so was really bad. I had to let the hurt in. But when I did, I was able to get healing I needed."

As human beings, we all experience pain, disappointment, and heartache at some point in our lives. These struggles can leave us feeling lost, alone, and hopeless. However, it's important to remember that it's okay to be hurting. In fact, it's a natural part of the human experience. The paradox is that, hiding from or trying to get away from the pain will cause the pain to continue. However, when we let it in with the help of the Lord and with safe people on our life team, that allows us to begin the true healing process.

God understands our pain and is patient with us as we work through our struggles. He is always with us, even in the darkest moments of our lives. When we turn to Him in prayer, He listens and offers us comfort and guidance. It's important to allow ourselves the time and space we need to heal. We may need to grieve, process, and work through our emotions before we can fully move forward. This is a necessary part of the healing process, and God understands that it takes time.

As we heal, we can find comfort in God's promises. He promises to be close to the brokenhearted and to save those who are crushed in spirit. He promises to heal our wounds and to make us whole again. We can trust in Him and His plan for our lives.

In the midst of our pain, it can be easy to feel alone and isolated. However, we must remember that we are not alone. We can lean on our loved ones for support and turn to our faith for guidance. God is patient with us and allows us to have the time we need to process and heal.

What is something that you need to heal from that you have been avoiding?

What are the next steps for you to begin the journey of healing?

Prayer:

Dear God, thank you for your love and patience with us as we go through the struggles of life. Help us to lean on you for comfort and guidance during difficult times. Give us the strength to heal and to trust in your promises. May we find peace and wholeness in your loving embrace. Amen.

CRIES THAT DRAW US NEAR

Psalm 34:17-18 (NASB) "The righteous cry, and the LORD hears And delivers them out of all their troubles. The LORD is near to the brokenhearted And saves those who are crushed in spirit."

About a year ago, a woman from my church shared a story where she was driving home and saw some kittens. She decided to flip around and try to find them. When she got to the park she asked the Lord, "If you want me to find them, please make them cry out so I can hear them."

Sometimes the Lord allows us to go through things so we will cry out so the right person will come to our aid. Also so we will cry out to Him.

We all face difficult times in life. Sometimes these trials are small and easily overcome, while other times they seem insurmountable. It's during these times that we can feel lost, alone, and abandoned. However, as Christians, we know that we are never truly alone. God is always with us, and He is always willing to help us through our trials.

In Psalm 34, the author reminds us that when we cry out to God, He hears us. He is close to the brokenhearted and saves those who are crushed in spirit. It's important to remember that God doesn't always take away our troubles, but He is always with us and will help us through them.

When we cry out to God, we are acknowledging that we cannot face our trials alone. We are admitting our weakness and need for His help. And just like the father in the parable of the prodigal son, God doesn't wait for us to be repentant before He comes to our aid. He is always waiting for us to cry out to Him, and when we do, He comes running to us.

So if you are going through a difficult time, don't be afraid to cry out to God. He hears you, and He is close to you. He will help you through your trials and be with you every step of the way.

Are you going through something right now?

Find someone who is safe that you can trust, give them a call and share what you're facing. If you're doing okay, Check in on those who you mentor or do life with.

Prayer:

Dear Lord, we thank you that you are always with us, even in our most difficult times. Help us to remember that we can cry out to you for help, and that you will always hear us. We ask for your help and guidance as we face our trials, and we pray that you would give us the strength to persevere. Thank you for your love and faithfulness, and for always being there for us. In Jesus' name we pray, Amen.

BE THE ABRAHAM GENERATION

Genesis 12:1-4 (NIV) The Lord had said to Abram, "Go from your country, your people and your father's household to the land I will show you.
"I will make you into a great nation, and I will bless you;
I will make your name great, and you will be a blessing.
I will bless those who bless you, and whoever curses you I will curse; and all peoples on earth will be blessed through you.
So Abram went, as the Lord had told him; and Lot went with him. Abram was seventy-five years old when he set out from Harran.

As Christians, we are called to be set apart from the world and to pursue a life of righteousness. In the Bible, we see numerous examples of individuals who chose to leave their past behind and start something new with God. One such example is Abraham.

In Genesis 12:1-4, we read about how God called Abram (later known as Abraham) to leave his country, his people, and his father's household and go to the land that God would show him. God promised to bless him and make him into a great nation. Abram obeyed and set out on his journey, not knowing where God was leading him.

As we read this story, we can learn a lot from Abraham. He was willing to leave his past behind and start fresh with God. He had faith in God's promises, even though he didn't fully understand how they would come to pass. Abraham's obedience to God paved the way for him to become the father of many nations.

Sometimes, we may find ourselves in a similar situation as Abraham. We may feel like we need to leave behind the ungodly influences of our past and start fresh with God. It may be difficult, but if we trust in God's promises and follow His leading, He will guide us and bless us.

We must also be willing to be the Abraham generation for others. We need to be willing to take a stand for what is right and follow God, even if it means going against the norm. We need to be the ones who set an example for others to follow and inspire them to pursue righteousness.

As we seek to be the Abraham generation, let us remember that we can do all things through Christ who strengthens us (Philippians 4:13). We do not have to rely on our own strength or understanding, but we can trust in God to lead us and empower us to do His will.

What is the call on your life?

Are you prepared to go after God's call even if it goes against popular culture?

Prayer

Heavenly Father, we thank You for the example of Abraham and his faithfulness to You. Help us to follow in his footsteps and be willing to leave behind our past and start fresh with You. Give us the courage to stand for what is right and to be the example for others to follow. We ask for Your guidance and strength as we seek to be the Abraham generation. In Jesus' name, we pray, Amen.

FOLLOW THE FAITHFUL

Hebrews 13:7,(NLT) "Remember your leaders who taught you the word of God. Think of all the good that has come from their lives, and follow the example of their faith."

About a decade ago, I was working for a friend who was looking at buying a piece of land. He asked if I would go with him to pray over the property. As we were walking, we came to a very large area, well over an acre of land covered in what we call California Grass. California Grass in Hawaii is infamous because it has these tiny hairs that are like fiberglass in your skin. Because I didn't want to be itchy for the next couple days, I walked directly behind him touching his back. He was parting the grass and it was folding back behind me.

Sometimes that is how we need to be when we are learning and going on our journey after the Lord. Similar to having a mentor, we can follow the example of those around us, but we need to remember that the only person we model our life after in the end is Jesus.

We all need someone to look up to, someone to follow, and someone to model our lives after. In the Bible, we see this time and time again. Elisha followed Elijah, Timothy followed Paul, and the disciples followed Jesus. By following someone else, we get to learn from their experiences and see firsthand what it means to live a life of faith.

When we follow someone who is faithful, we get to witness the power of God at work. We don't have to blindly jump into the unknown and hope for the best. We get to see how our mentor trusts in God and relies on Him through every step of their journey. We get to see their faith in action, and as a result, our own faith is increased.

Surrounding ourselves with those who are willing to risk it all for the sake of the Gospel is essential. These people inspire us to take bold steps of faith ourselves. They challenge us to step out of our comfort zones and trust God, even when it's scary. We need to follow the faithful, those who are living their lives in complete surrender to God.

But following someone else doesn't mean we blindly accept everything they say or do. We must use discernment and judge everything by the Word of God. Not everyone who claims to be a leader or mentor is truly faithful to God. We must be careful who we follow and make sure they are leading us closer to God and not away from Him.

Let's choose to follow those who are faithfully following Christ. Let's surround ourselves with people who are willing to risk it all for the sake of the Gospel. And let's continue to grow in our faith as we witness the power of God at work in the lives of those we look up to. May we also be an example of faith to those who are following us.

Who are you following in your life right now? Do you have a mentor? Is there a particular person in the bible who you identify with?

Prayer:

Dear Lord, help us to follow the faithful, those who are living their lives in complete surrender to You. Give us discernment to judge everything by Your Word, and help us to surround ourselves with people who are leading us closer to You. Increase our faith as we witness Your power at work in the lives of those we look up to. And may we also be an example of faith to those who are following us. In Jesus' name, Amen.

THE POWER OF THE WORD

1 Corinthians 4:20 (NIV) - "For the kingdom of God is not in word but in power."

Why is it that for so many we are able to feel strong emotions about the scriptures regarding the law, but are unable to keep that so energy when it comes to the scriptures about God's love for us. The words of law have incredible power, but the words of God on Love are absolute. The scriptures are God breathed.

We need to remember not to cherry pick scriptures that match our world view, yes we must go deep into the study and understand all aspects but we also mustn't try to bend passages in order to work with what we believe. This is both positive and negative, if we have a very negative view of ourselves, it's easy to see scriptures that condemn our actions.

We often hear the phrase "actions speak louder than words," but as Christians, we must remember that words can also have power. However, without the power of the Holy Spirit behind them, they are just empty words. In 1 Corinthians 4:20, Paul reminds us that the kingdom of God is not just in words but in power. We need the power of the Holy Spirit to bring life to the words we speak.

As Christians, we have been given the privilege of sharing the Word of God with others. But it's not enough to just share the words, we must also demonstrate the power of those words through our lives. People need to see the transformation that takes place when the Word is applied with the power of the Holy Spirit.

Rules and laws provide a clear framework for behavior, whereas the words of love require us to take a step of faith and trust in the power of the Holy Spirit to transform us from the inside out.

We must be willing to allow the Holy Spirit to work in us so that our words are not just empty, but are accompanied by the power of God. When we allow the Holy Spirit to work in us, we become vessels of His power and love, and our words become life-giving to those who hear them.

Are you missing part of the scriptures in your life?

Have you been utilizing the full power of the scriptures? To bring correction, to bring healing, to express love?

Prayer:

Father, we thank you for the power of your Word. Help us to be vessels of your power and love so that our words are not just empty, but are accompanied by the power of your Holy Spirit. May we be willing to allow you to work in us so that we can be effective witnesses for your kingdom. In Jesus' name, Amen.

THE IMMEASURABLE
LOVE OF GOD

1 Corinthians 13:13 (NASB) - "But now faith, hope, and love, abide these three; but the greatest of these is love."

An older man shared his testimony with me, a story of tragedy and heartbreak that was very difficult to hear. He experienced a large amount of abuse as a child at the hand of his parents, and a few others he was supposed to be loved and protected by. As he got older, the natural path followed of bad choices and incarceration. At a point where he was on the precipice of making some final decisions, there was an old woman from one of the churches in his town who ended up meeting him and becoming a part of his life. She gave him the one thing no one has done before, Love. She invited him into her home and helped him to find a job and turn his life around.

He was a completely different person because he had one touch of the Fathers love through a faithful woman.

Love is a powerful force that can transform our lives in ways we never imagined. It is a force that can break down barriers, heal wounds, and bring people together. Love is the foundation of all good things and the essence of God himself.

The power of love is immeasurable, and it is through the love of God that we are able to experience the fullness of life. When we experience the love of God, we are transformed and renewed. It is a love that is unconditional and never-ending.

In John 15:13, Jesus says, "Greater love has no one than this: to lay down one's life for one's friends." This is the ultimate expression of love and sacrifice, and it is through this act that we are able to experience the full power of love.

Love is not just a feeling, it is an action. We are called to love others as God loves us, and to show that love through our actions. We must be willing to lay down our own lives for others, just as Jesus did for us. It is through this sacrificial love that we are able to experience the power of love and transform the world around us.

Have you spent time with the Lord to experience His love?

Is there someone who you can show love to? Someone who maybe doesn't "Deserve" it or someone who is difficult to love.

Prayer:

Dear God, thank you for the immeasurable power of your love. Help us to love others as you love us, and to show that love through our actions. May your love transform our lives and the world around us. Amen.

THE HOPE OF GLORY WITHIN US

Colossians 1:27 (NIV) - "To them God has chosen to make known among the Gentiles the glorious riches of this mystery, which is Christ in you, the hope of glory."

I was watching a video where they were unclogging a commercial sized storm drain. I'll be honest the video was pretty gross. They used a special system to force out a huge amount of compacted mud and debris. Once they did, the rain water flowed very clear and very, very fast.

As believers in Christ, we have the hope of glory within us - the hope of eternal life and the promise of God's presence and power in our lives. But sometimes we can feel spiritually clogged up just like the drain pipe. When we allow sin, doubt, fear, and worry to consume our hearts and minds, we create a barrier that prevents the Holy Spirit from flowing freely within us. We are unable to share the love, joy, and peace of Christ with those around us.

But the good news is that we can always turn to Jesus and ask Him to cleanse and renew us. When we repent and turn away from sin, He washes us clean and fills us with His Spirit. When we surrender our worries and fears to Him, He replaces them with His peace that surpasses all understanding.

When we allow Christ to flow freely within us, we become vessels of His love and power. We can share His hope with others and be a light in a dark world. We can be used by God to bring healing, restoration, and transformation to those around us.
So let us daily invite Christ to work in us and through us. Let us ask Him to remove anything that clogs up our hearts and prevents us from experiencing the fullness of His love and power. Let us be vessels of hope and glory in a world that so desperately needs it.

What's got your heart clogged these days?

What are your next steps to get that gunk out of you?

Prayer:

Dear Jesus, thank you for being the hope of glory within me.
I ask that you cleanse me of anything that clogs up my heart
and prevents your Spirit from flowing freely within me. Fill
me with your love, joy, peace, and power. Help me to be a
vessel of hope and glory to those around me. In your name, I
pray. Amen.

EVERYONE HAS A ROLE

"Each of you should use whatever gift you have received to serve others, as faithful stewards of God's grace in its various forms." - 1 Peter 4:10 (NIV)

The number of times I have used my knife as a prying tool or a screw driver because I didn't want to simply to my tool box to get a prybar or screwdriver… It's truly embarrassing. That said, the number of times I have slipped and cut myself – you would assume it's non-habit forming but I keep doing it. For some reason, I never learn to just go get the right tool for the right job.

In the Old Testament, only the priest was allowed to burn incense in the tabernacle or temple. It was a holy task, set apart for a specific group of people who had been chosen by God for that role. In the same way, God has given each of us specific gifts and talents to use for His kingdom. We are not meant to take on someone else's purpose or try to do everything ourselves.

When we try to take on too much, we can become overwhelmed and burned out. God has given each of us a specific role to play, and when we focus on fulfilling that role, we can experience true joy and fulfillment in serving Him. We don't have to be everything to everyone, but we can use our unique gifts and talents to serve those around us and bring glory to God.

Sometimes, we may feel like our role is not as important as someone else's. We may envy those who seem to have a more prominent role or a more significant impact. However, God sees the value in each of us and the specific roles He has given us to play in His kingdom. We should focus on using our gifts to the best of our ability and trust that God will use them for His purposes.

As we serve in our specific roles, we can also encourage and support those around us in their roles. We are all part of the same body of Christ, and each part is necessary for the body to function properly. When we work together and use our gifts and talents to serve each other, we can experience the fullness of God's kingdom.

What is your gifting?

What are you doing to steward your gift to bring glory with excellence?

Prayer:

Dear God, thank you for the unique gifts and talents you have given each of us. Help us to focus on fulfilling the roles you have given us and to trust that you will use them for your purposes. Show us how to encourage and support those around us in their roles and work together to bring glory to your name. In Jesus' name, we pray. Amen.

GRATTITUDE FOR THE ORDINARY

1 Thessalonians 5:18 (AMP) - "In every situation [no matter what the circumstances] be thankful and continually give thanks to God; for this is the will of God for you in Christ Jesus."

Once I was working as a project manager for a construction company. I had a crew of around 7 people at the time. One day I had the thought, I have spent all of my encouragement for when the guys do something extraordinary. Which of course is well deserved, but what happens if I honor a person for just being, doing what they are supposed to do? I was taught by a superior, "Why would you tell them good job? All they did was what we pay them for." I really didn't like that, many times in life we miss out on the opportunity to build relationship, and encourage people when we don't speak up.

It's easy to take things for granted, especially when they're part of someone's job or routine. We often only express gratitude when someone goes above and beyond what we expect. But what about the things that are simply part of their job? It's important to show gratitude for those as well.

When we express gratitude for the ordinary things that people do, it can be a powerful way to encourage and uplift them. It lets them know that their work is noticed and appreciated, and that they're making a difference in someone's life.

And it's not just about making someone else feel good. When we cultivate an attitude of gratitude, it changes our own perspective and outlook on life. We become more aware of the good things around us, and more appreciative of the people who make them happen.

So let's take the time to thank the people in our lives for the things they do, even if they're just doing their job. Let's show them that they're valued and appreciated, and encourage them to continue to do their best.

Let's make gratitude a habit in our lives, not just for the big things, but for the ordinary things as well. May we cultivate a heart of thankfulness and encourage those around us to do the same. And may we always remember that every good thing comes from God, and give thanks to Him in all circumstances.

Find someone in your life who you can tell them that they are doing a good job and that you are grateful for them.

Prayer:
Dear God, thank you for the people in our lives who do the ordinary things that make our lives better. Help us to show them our gratitude and appreciation, and to encourage them in their work. May we cultivate a spirit of thankfulness and give thanks to You in all circumstances, knowing that every good thing comes from You. In Jesus' name we pray, amen.

IT'S NOT A TONGUE PROBLEM IT'S A HEART PROBLEM

"The good person out of the good treasure of his heart produces good, and the evil person out of his evil treasure produces evil, for out of the abundance of the heart his mouth speaks." - Luke 6:45 (ESV)

I was watching the first Marvel Avengers movie, throughout the movie, Iron Man asks the Hulk, what is your secret? Before the final fight scene the Hulk character says, "That's my secret, I'm always angry."

I resonated with that line so deeply. Growing up, I was always afraid to get drunk because I was worried that if the barrier that I forced up, was taken down, someone would get hurt, thus I have never gotten drunk. I had so much anger bottled up and pressed down, very small things could spark a very large and angry reaction.

It took years of work, but I realized over time, that it was easier to deal with the anger than it was to just try to hide it and keep myself in check 100% of the time.

Have you ever struggled with controlling your tongue? Perhaps you have said things in the heat of the moment that you later regretted. Or maybe you find yourself constantly biting your tongue to avoid speaking words of anger or criticism.

The truth is, our tongue problem is not really a tongue problem at all. It's a heart problem. As Luke 6:45 tells us, what we say is simply an overflow of what is in our hearts. If our hearts are filled with anger, bitterness, or jealousy, it will inevitably come out in our words.

But when we allow God to transform our hearts, our words will also be transformed. As we fill our hearts with God's love, joy, and peace, our mouths will overflow with words of kindness, encouragement, and grace.

When we make a conscious effort to fill our hearts with God's goodness, our words will naturally reflect that goodness. But this transformation doesn't happen overnight. It takes time, effort, and a willingness to surrender our hearts to God.

So today, let's ask God to transform our hearts and help us control our tongues. Let's choose to speak words of love, kindness, and grace, even when it's difficult. And let's thank God for the power of his transforming love that can change our hearts and our words.

Do you have hidden things that you need to deal with?

Spend some time with the Lord as David did and ask God to search your heart.

Prayer:

Dear God, we confess that we have struggled with controlling our tongues. We ask for your forgiveness and for your help in transforming our hearts. Fill us with your love, joy, and peace, so that our words may overflow with goodness and grace. Help us to speak words of love and encouragement to those around us, and to honor you with everything we say. In Jesus' name, amen.

THE INHERATANCE OF THE FAITHUFL

Luke 15:11-32 (NIV)

"The older brother became angry and refused to go in. So his father went out and pleaded with him. But he answered his father, 'Look! All these years I've been slaving for you and never disobeyed your orders. Yet you never gave me even a young goat so I could celebrate with my friends. But when this son of yours who has squandered your property with prostitutes comes home, you kill the fattened calf for him!'

"'My son,' the father said, 'you are always with me, and everything I have is yours. But we had to celebrate and be glad, because this brother of yours was dead and is alive again; he was lost and is found.'"

When I was around 13 years old, I desperately wanted a Lamborghini. I came from a very poor family and I had no idea that my request was probably the same as asking for a trip to the moon. My mom was so sweet and sassy, she kept telling me she got me a purple Lambo for my birthday and would say things like, "It's on the fourth floor."

For that birthday we went to a performance called Legends in Concert, I was also a huge fan of Michael Jackson. My sister who worked for the show, got the Michael Jackson impersonator to announce from the stage that it was my birthday and he also gave me a signed montage that he made for me because he knew I was a fan. But when the birthday cake came out with a toy Lamborghini on it, my mom said, "See we got you a Lamborghini." Because of my deep disappointment I was very sour and unappreciative.

It took a while for me to forgive myself because of how sad I felt when I realized how ungrateful I was. I got to go to an amazing performance, my favorite performer dedicated it to me, I was with my family friends, the food was good, the cake was delicious and I got a cool toy car plus presents. How could I not be more excited about that?

In the parable of the prodigal son, we often focus on the younger son who left and squandered his fortune. But there is another character in the story who is equally important: the older son who stayed faithful to his father.

The older son worked hard and was loyal to his father, yet he didn't receive the same kind of celebration as the younger son did upon his return. In fact, he was resentful and angry that his father had never given him a fattened calf to feast with his friends. But what he failed to realize was that everything his father owned was technically his inheritance because he was the one who stayed.

The father tells his older son, "Everything I have is yours" (Luke 15:31). The older son didn't have to leave to inherit everything his father had; he just had to remain faithful.

In the same way, it is so easy for us to miss out on the amazing blessings we have because we are so fixated on the things that we don't have.

So let us stay faithful and focused on God, trusting in his promises and resting in the assurance that we are his beloved children and heirs of his kingdom.

What are you grateful for?

Spend some time to come up with a list of the things you do have so you can shift your focus.

Prayer:

Dear God, thank you for the inheritance we have in you as faithful children. Help us to stay focused on you and trust in your promises. May we not be envious or jealous of others, but rather rejoice in the blessings you have given us. We love you and praise you, now and forever. Amen.

ALWAYS ON A MISSION TRIP

John 15:19 (ESV) - "If the world hates you, know that it has hated me before it hated you. If you were of the world, the world would love you as its own; but because you are not of the world, but I chose you out of the world, therefore the world hates you."

Recently I was on a trip to Europe, when I got home I was so excited to share pictures and tell stories. When you are on vacation or a mission trip, there's often something that just feels magical while you are there. While sharing one of the stories, I had the revelation that I was very excited to share what happened in the distant land that was not my home. The bible says that we are not of this world. So why am I not more excited about the things I experience in day to day life since it is not my home?

As believers, we are called to be in the world but not of the world. We are chosen by Jesus to be His ambassadors and to share His love with those around us. This means that wherever we go, we are called to be a light in the darkness.

Instead of waiting for a mission trip to come around, let's take every opportunity to share the love of Jesus with those we encounter on a daily basis. Whether it's through a kind word or a listening ear, we can show the love of Jesus to those around us.

And when we spend time with the Lord in our daily devotions, we can share with Him about our "mission trip" experiences. We can tell Him about the conversations we had and the ways we were able to share His love with others. He delights in hearing about His children spreading His love to the world.

Let's shift our thinking and start living our lives as if we are always on a mission trip. Let's be intentional about sharing the love of Jesus with those around us and take every opportunity to be a light in the darkness.

Prayer:

Heavenly Father, thank You for choosing us to be Your ambassadors in the world. Help us to live our lives with the mindset that we are always on a mission trip, ready to share Your love with those around us. Give us the courage to step out in faith and be a light in the darkness. We love You and praise You. In Jesus' name, Amen.

WALKING THROUGH THE MESS WITH GRACE

"Therefore, since we have been justified by faith, we have peace with God through our Lord Jesus Christ. Through him we have also obtained access by faith into this grace in which we stand, and we rejoice in hope of the glory of God. Not only that, but we rejoice in our sufferings, knowing that suffering produces endurance, and endurance produces character, and character produces hope" - Romans 5:1-4 (ESV)

When it comes to being clean, personally I can be obsessed. When I was younger I used to shower 3-4 times per day. Yes, I have changed since then, specifically one of the moments that made me change was a time I went hiking after a big rain. For some reason, I don't know why to this day, we decided to go hiking the day after a very big rain. As you would imagine, I got muddy fairly early. I so desperately wanted to stop hiking and take a box of cleaning towels and get all the mud off of me.

At the behest of my friend I just kept hiking. It was very difficult at first to just keep going since I was covered with mud. However, we made it to the waterfall and got to enjoy one of my favorite views.

Life can be messy. We can find ourselves in situations where we feel overwhelmed, confused, and hopeless. In these moments, we may cry out to God for help and expect Him to immediately remove the mess from our lives. However, our yes to Jesus doesn't necessarily mean that He will automatically wipe away the mess. Instead, it means that He will provide us with the grace to walk through it.

The grace of God is a powerful force that sustains us in the midst of trials and tribulations. It is the unmerited favor of God that enables us to endure through difficult times. When we say yes to Jesus, we are saying yes to the grace that He provides. We are saying yes to the peace that surpasses all understanding, the joy that comes in the morning, and the hope that we have in Him.

As we walk through the mess, we may feel weak and helpless. However, the Apostle Paul reminds us that in our weaknesses, God's strength is made perfect. When we are at our lowest, God is at His highest. We can rest in the assurance that His grace is sufficient for us, and His power is made perfect in our weaknesses.

Walking through the mess with grace is not always easy. It requires us to surrender our own wills and desires to God and trust in His plan for our lives. It requires us to lean into His grace and allow Him to work in and through us. It requires us to persevere through the pain and trust that He will bring beauty from ashes.

Our yes to Jesus doesn't necessarily mean that He will automatically wipe away the mess from our lives. However, it means that He will provide us with the grace to walk through it. Let us lean into His grace and trust in His plan for our lives, knowing that in our weaknesses, He is strong. Let us rejoice in our sufferings, knowing that they produce endurance, character, and hope. And let us walk through the mess with grace, knowing that God is with us every step of the way.

How can you keep going amidst the mess to draw closer to God?

How can you begin to let go of things going on the journey of healing?

Prayer:

Heavenly Father, we thank You for Your grace that sustains us through the mess of life. Help us to trust in Your plan for our lives and lean into Your grace. Strengthen us in our weaknesses and help us to persevere through the trials and tribulations of life. May we rejoice in our sufferings, knowing that they produce endurance, character, and hope. And may we walk through the mess with grace, knowing that You are with us every step of the way. In Jesus' name, we pray, Amen.

FOLLOWING JESUS
TO OUR DESTINY

"Then Jesus said to his disciples, 'Whoever wants to be my disciple must deny themselves and take up their cross and follow me. For whoever wants to save their life will lose it, but whoever loses their life for me will find it. What good will it be for someone to gain the whole world, yet forfeit their soul? Or what can anyone give in exchange for their soul?'" - Matthew 16:24-26 (NIV)

A few years ago, I was asked to teach a couple of entry level classes at a university here in Hawaii. I hemmed and hawed about the thought for so long because of a lot of insecure questions and self-doubt, that the position was given to someone else. Now It's possible that it wasn't for me in the long run, but I will never know because I waited and waited to decide.

As followers of Jesus, we are called to deny ourselves, take up our cross, and follow Him. This means that we surrender our will and desires to follow the path that Jesus has for us. He has a plan and a purpose for our lives, and it is our job to trust Him and obey Him.

However, sometimes we miss the call that Jesus has for us. Maybe we are too focused on our own plans or distracted by the world around us. We might even hear the call, but we come up with excuses or reasons why we can't answer it. And when we do finally answer the call, we often bring our baggage and refuse to let it go, hindering our journey to our destiny.

Jesus never promised us an easy journey, but He did promise us that if we lose our life for His sake, we will find it. He has a destiny and purpose for each of us, and it is up to us to trust Him and follow Him.

Missing the Call: Sometimes we miss the call that Jesus has for us because we are too busy focusing on our own plans or caught up in the distractions of the world. When we are not listening to Jesus, we can miss out on the amazing things that He has planned for our lives.

Giving Excuses: Other times, we hear the call that Jesus has for us, but we come up with excuses or reasons why we can't answer it. We might feel like we are not qualified, or we might think that we are too busy. However, when we give excuses, we are missing out on the opportunity to be part of something greater than ourselves.

Bringing Our Baggage: Finally, even when we do answer the call that Jesus has for us, we often bring our baggage with us. We hold onto things that we should let go of, hindering our journey to our destiny. We need to trust Jesus and let go of our past hurts and mistakes, so that we can move forward and fulfill our purpose.

As we follow Jesus to our destiny, let us remember to listen for His call, answer it without hesitation or excuse, and let go of our baggage. Jesus has a plan and purpose for each of our lives, and when we trust Him and obey Him, we will experience a life full of joy and fulfillment.

Have you been ignoring phone calls from the Lord?

What is the thing that the Lord is telling you to do, that you know you are supposed to do but just haven't gone after it yet?

Prayer:

Dear Lord, help us to listen for Your call and to answer it without hesitation or excuse. Help us to let go of our baggage so that we can fulfill the destiny and purpose that You have for our lives. Thank You for always leading us down the path that is best for us. In Jesus' name, Amen.

THE BLESSING OF VALLEYS

Psalm 23:4 (NIV)- "Even though I walk through the darkest valley, I will fear no evil, for you are with me; your rod and your staff, they comfort me."

Being born and raised in Hawaii, it is so easy to take it's natural beauty for granted. I have had the pleasure of working with organizations that bring in a lot of foreigners. As a result, I have had the opportunity to take them hiking on some of our beautiful trails. One day we were hiking through the valley and one of the Europeans stopped and exclaimed, "Danny! Can you believe that you get to live here?!?" It was in that moment I looked around and realized that although the top of some of the mountain was a little dried out, the valley was lush and green with beautiful tropical flowers.

We often look at valleys as places to avoid. They are deep, dark and difficult to navigate. We often try to find ways to avoid them and get to the mountaintop. However, what we fail to realize is that the valleys have their own blessings.

In Psalm 23:4, the Psalmist declares that even though he walks through the darkest valley, he will fear no evil, for God is with him. The valley represents a place of challenge, difficulty, and struggle. But it is also the place where the Psalmist finds comfort in God's presence. The valley is a place of growth and transformation.

Sometimes, we need to go through the valley to receive the blessings that God has in store for us. In the valley, we learn to depend on God and trust Him even when things are difficult. It is in the valley that we discover our strength and resilience. We learn to hold on to hope and keep our faith even in the midst of trials.

In the valley, we also find refreshing water and fertile ground. The valleys are often where the rivers and streams flow, providing life to the plants and animals around them. The plants grow and bear fruit in the valley. In the same way, the valley can be a place of growth and abundance for us. We can discover new opportunities, relationships, and experiences that we would not have encountered on the mountaintop.

So, let us not fear the valley but embrace it as a place of growth and transformation. Let us trust in God's guidance and provision in every season of our lives. May we find the blessings that the valley holds for us and grow stronger in our faith through every trial.

Are you in a valley? Take a look around and find the beauty in where you are.

Lord, help us to trust in your guidance even in the midst of the valleys of our lives. Help us to see the blessings that these challenging times hold for us. Give us the strength to walk through the valleys with faith and courage. May we find your presence and comfort in every trial. Amen

ENDURANCE THROUGH PATIENCE AND JOY

Colossians 1:11-14 (NLT) We also pray that you will be strengthened with all his glorious power so you will have all the endurance and patience you need. May you be filled with joy, always thanking the Father. He has enabled you to share in the inheritance that belongs to his people, who live in the light. For he has rescued us from the kingdom of darkness and transferred us into the Kingdom of his dear Son, who purchased our freedom and forgave our sins.

Have you ever sat through a meeting and it droned on and on. Your patience grows thin, you nearly say things that you don't mean. You may feel exhausted and frustrated. That's something that is easy to feel when we are not happy about what we have to do.

How about a great date with someone you really care about? Have you noticed how fast the time goes by? How much things can go wrong but yet you still have the capacity for it? When we are happy about things, we are able to endure much. However the bible tells us to have joy, not happiness. Joy is from the Lord, and as such is not dependent or even related to our circumstances.

In Colossians 1:11-14, Paul prays for the Colossian believers to be strengthened with all His glorious power so that they can have endurance and patience, filled with joy and always thanking the Father. This passage is a beautiful reminder of the grace that God has given to us through Jesus Christ.

As Christians, we are not promised an easy life. In fact, Jesus told His disciples that in this world, we will have trouble (John 16:33). But God gives us the strength to endure through any trial or hardship that we may face. When we feel weak and helpless, we can turn to God for the power we need to keep going.

Patience is also a crucial element of our faith. We may not always understand why God allows certain things to happen in our lives, but we can trust that He has a plan and a purpose for everything. By patiently waiting on Him, we can see His hand at work in our lives and trust that He will work all things together for our good (Romans 8:28).

Finally, we can be filled with joy because of the incredible inheritance that we have in Christ. We have been rescued from the kingdom of darkness and transferred into the Kingdom of His dear Son. Jesus purchased our freedom and forgave our sins, and because of that, we have the hope of eternal life with Him.

Let us remember to seek God for the strength we need to endure, the patience to wait on His timing, and the joy that comes from knowing Him. May we always be thankful for the inheritance we have in Christ and the freedom that He has given us.

Since Joy is a choice, how can you choose Joy today?

Prayer:

Dear Heavenly Father, we thank You for the incredible grace and power that You have given us through Your Son, Jesus Christ. We pray that You would strengthen us with all Your glorious power so that we may have endurance and patience through any trial or hardship. Fill us with joy as we remember the inheritance we have in Christ and the freedom that He has given us. We thank You and praise You for all that You have done and all that You will continue to do in our lives. In Jesus' name, Amen.

FAITH THAT FLIPS
THE WORLD

Acts 17:6 (NKJV) - "But when they did not find them, they dragged Jason and some brethren to the rulers of the city, crying out, "These who have turned the world upside down have come here too."

The book of Acts recounts the story of Paul and Silas who, while on their missionary journey, were met with opposition and persecution. They were often accused of causing trouble and disturbance wherever they went, but this did not deter them from their mission. In fact, they saw it as an opportunity to spread the message of Christ to more people.

As Christians, we too are called to be agents of change in the world. We are to be fearless in our faith and willing to disturb the status quo. This means that we will not always be accepted by everyone, and we may even be met with resistance and persecution. However, just as Paul and Silas did not allow these challenges to hinder their mission, we too must persevere in the face of opposition.

Our faith should be contagious, causing a disturbance in the lives of those around us. We should be so full of the love and power of Christ that it spills over into every area of our lives, disrupting the status quo and turning the world upside down. When we are unashamed of our faith and boldly proclaim the truth of the Gospel, people will take notice and some may even come to know Christ through our witness.

As we live out our faith in a world that is often hostile to it, let us remember that we are not called to blend in, but to stand out. We are to be salt and light in a world that desperately needs it. May our lives cause a disturbance that leads others to Christ.

Do the demons tremble when you start driving through their town?

Are you willing to take the risk of talking to someone who you wouldn't normally?

Prayer:

Dear Lord, give us the courage to be agents of change in the world. Help us to be fearless in our faith and willing to disturb the status quo for the sake of the Gospel. May our lives be a witness to your love and power, and may others come to know you through our witness. We pray this in Jesus' name. Amen.

GOD'S OWN CHILD

Galatians 4:7 (NLT) - "Now you are no longer a slave but God's own child. And since you are his child, God has made you his heir."

How many of you knew a bully in school? I wasn't a
particularly big child, nor was I all that tough. So I got
bullied when I was young. Particularly I was bullied by
someone much older than me. He was a typical bully,
older and angry for no reason. He used to hold me over
the balcony when I was probably 8 or 9. I was so
terrified of him, one day I finally told my dad about it
and he talked to the guy and he left me alone after that.
Nevertheless I was still afraid of him long after my
father talked to him, long after I didn't see him.

One day, when I was a full grown adult. I was sitting in
a coffee shop and in walked the former bully. In the
first moment I saw him I could feel the slight shudder of
fear. The slight drop in the pit of my stomach. Then the
fear turned into anger. I am just under 6' tall and heavy
enough. He apparently was always about 5'6 or 5'7 and
not very big. After a few minutes I realized that I have
been through so much more and dealt with much more
dangerous people since I was a child.   Then I realized I
don't need to have any feelings toward him, there were
plenty of reasons for him to be angry and try to bully
those around him. I was able to not feel, angry, sad or
mad at him.

When we come to Jesus and surrender our lives to Him,
we are no longer slaves to sin and the things of this
world. We become children of God, and He becomes our
Father. And just like any good earthly father, God
provides for His children and wants the best for them. In
fact, as His children, we are not only provided for, but
we are also heirs to His kingdom.

As God's children, we are set apart and given a new
identity in Christ. We are no longer defined by our past
mistakes, our failures, or our shortcomings. We are
defined by who God says we are - loved, forgiven, and

redeemed. And because of this new identity, we have access to all the benefits of being a child of God.

One of those benefits is our inheritance. As God's children, we are heirs to His kingdom. This means that we have access to all the riches of heaven - the joy, peace, love, and grace that come from being in relationship with our heavenly Father. And while we may not see all of these benefits fully realized in this life, we can trust that they are waiting for us in eternity.

As we journey through this life, let us remember that we are not slaves to sin and the things of this world. We are God's own children, and as His children, we have access to all the benefits of being heirs to His kingdom. Let us walk in the confidence of knowing that we are loved, forgiven, and redeemed, and that our inheritance is waiting for us in eternity.

What are you holding onto that's holding you back?

Prayer

Heavenly Father, thank You for adopting us as Your own children and for making us heirs to Your kingdom. Help us to walk in the confidence of knowing who we are in You and to live in the freedom that comes from being Your children. May we always be mindful of our inheritance and look forward to the day when we will fully realize all of the benefits of being Your heirs. In Jesus' name, Amen.

NEVER GIVE UP PRAYING

Luke 18:1-5 (NIV) Then Jesus told his disciples a parable to show them that they should always pray and not give up. He said: "In a certain town there was a judge who neither feared God nor cared what people thought. And there was a widow in that town who kept coming to him with the plea, 'Grant me justice against my adversary.'

"For some time he refused. But finally he said to himself, 'Even though I don't fear God or care what people think, yet because this widow keeps bothering me, I will see that she gets justice, so that she won't eventually come and attack me!'"

In Luke 18:1-5, Jesus tells a parable about a widow who kept going to an unjust judge to seek justice against her adversary. The judge refused to listen to her for some time, but she persisted in her request. The judge eventually gave in to the widow's persistent pleas and granted her justice.

This parable teaches us the importance of persistence in prayer. The widow did not give up despite the judge's lack of interest and her persistence paid off in the end. Similarly, we should not give up on our prayers even when it seems like nothing is happening. We should keep praying and trust that God hears our prayers and will answer them in His perfect timing.

It is important to note that persistence in prayer does not mean we should pray just for the sake of praying. Our prayers should come from a sincere heart, seeking God's will and guidance in our lives. We should pray with faith and trust that God knows what is best for us and will answer our prayers according to His will.

When we persist in prayer, we demonstrate our trust and faith in God's power and love. We acknowledge that we cannot solve all our problems on our own and need His help. We also show our dependence on Him and His guidance in our lives.

We should never give up on our prayers. We should persist in prayer, trusting that God hears our prayers and will answer them according to His perfect will. Let us keep praying with faith, knowing that our persistence will pay off in the end.

Is there something that you are giving up on?

Prayer:

Dear God, help us to be persistent in prayer and to trust in Your power and love. Give us the faith to keep praying, even when it seems like nothing is happening. Help us to seek Your will and guidance in our lives and to trust that You know what is best for us. Thank you for hearing our prayers and for answering them according to Your perfect timing. In Jesus' name, we pray. Amen.

THE PROOF IN THE PUDDING

Matthew 11:2-6 (NIV) When John, who was in prison, heard about the deeds of the Messiah, he sent his disciples to ask him, "Are you the one who is to come, or should we expect someone else?"

Jesus replied, "Go back and report to John what you hear and see: The blind receive sight, the lame walk, those who have leprosy are cleansed, the deaf hear, the dead are raised, and the good news is proclaimed to the poor. Blessed is anyone who does not stumble on account of me."

John the Baptist, who had baptized Jesus and announced Him as the Messiah, found himself in prison and sent his disciples to ask Jesus a crucial question: "Are you the one who is to come, or should we expect someone else?" (Matthew 11:3). John needed reassurance that Jesus was the true Messiah, and not just another religious teacher or prophet.

Instead of answering directly, Jesus told John's disciples to report what they had seen and heard: "The blind receive sight, the lame walk, those who have leprosy are cleansed, the deaf hear, the dead are raised, and the good news is proclaimed to the poor" (Matthew 11:5). Jesus was saying that the proof of His identity as the Messiah was not just in what He said, but in what He did.

When I was younger, I struggled a lot with insecurity. In those days I needed to try to pretend that I was something special long before I had ever actually accomplished anything. I would say some of the craziest things just to feel valuable. I would respond to people with anger when they tried to question me because I was worried that they would figure out the truth.

As I got older, wiser and actually did things with my life, I no longer needed to try to prove things, didn't have to tell people I was good at something. I would just live my life, doing things the best I could.

This concept of the proof being in the pudding applies to us as well. We can say anything we want about ourselves or about others, but the proof is in our actions. Our words must be backed up by our deeds. It is not enough to say that we are Christians or that we believe in God; we must demonstrate our faith through our actions.

In the same way, when we encounter doubts and questions about our faith, we must look to the evidence of God's work in our lives and in the world around us. Just as Jesus pointed to the miraculous healings and the proclamation of the good news as evidence of His identity as the Messiah, we can look to the ways God has transformed our lives and the lives of others through His grace and love.

Let us not be like John the Baptist, who in a moment of doubt needed reassurance of Jesus' identity as the Messiah. Instead, let us have faith that is strong enough to weather any storm and trust in the evidence of God's work in our lives and in the world around us.

As we go about our day, let us remember that the proof is in the pudding. May our words be backed up by our deeds and may our faith be evident through our actions. Let us trust in the evidence of God's work in our lives and have faith that is strong enough to weather any storm.

Is there evidence of God's love in your life?

Prayer:

Dear God, help us to remember that the proof of our faith is in our actions. May we live our lives in a way that demonstrates our love for you and our commitment to following your ways. Strengthen our faith so that we may trust in the evidence of your work in our lives and in the world around us. In Jesus' name, Amen.

The Consequence of Disobedience

Zechariah 1:2-6 (NIV) "The Lord was very angry with your ancestors. Therefore tell the people: This is what the Lord Almighty says: 'Return to me,' declares the Lord Almighty, 'and I will return to you,' says the Lord Almighty. Do not be like your ancestors, to whom the earlier prophets proclaimed: This is what the Lord Almighty says: 'Turn from your evil ways and your evil practices.' But they would not listen or pay attention to me, declares the Lord. Where are your ancestors now? And the prophets, do they live forever? But did not my words and my decrees, which I commanded my servants the prophets, overtake your ancestors?
"Then they repented and said, 'The Lord Almighty has done to us what our ways and practices deserve, just as he determined to do.'"

When I was about 8 years old, my family and some of our family friends went to the beach to have a BBQ. A couple of the younger boys and I were walking around a tree and the younger brother said, only I can walk here because I have my slippers on. I being stubborn and not being willing to listen to someone around 4 or 5 years younger than me ignored his warning. Immediately after I walked through hot coals.

Throughout the Bible, there are numerous examples of warnings given to the people of God about the consequences of disobedience. One such warning is found in the book of Zechariah. The prophet Zechariah was sent to the exiles who had returned to Jerusalem to rebuild the temple. He urged them to return to the Lord and warned them of the judgment that would come if they refused.

In Zechariah 1:2-6, the Lord says to the people, "Return to me, and I will return to you... Do not be like your ancestors, to whom the earlier prophets proclaimed: This is what the Lord Almighty says: 'Turn from your evil ways and your evil practices.' But they would not listen or pay attention to me, declares the Lord." The Lord had warned the people of Israel through the prophets, but they refused to listen.

Just like the story of walking through the coals, we can often be tempted to ignore the warnings of others, even those who are younger or seemingly less experienced. But the consequences of disobedience can be severe. The people of Israel suffered greatly because they refused to heed the warnings of the prophets.

Similarly, we must be careful to discern who and what we listen to. There are many voices in the world today, and not all of them are speaking the truth. We must turn to the Word of God for guidance and wisdom. The Bible is filled with warnings and instructions for living a godly life.

As we seek to follow God, let us remember the warnings of the prophets and the consequences of disobedience. Let us turn to the Lord with repentant hearts and seek His guidance in all things. May we have ears to hear and hearts that are open to His truth.

God's Warnings Are For Our Good

The warnings that God gives us are not meant to harm us or restrict us, but rather to protect us and guide us. God loves us and wants what is best for us, and His warnings are a reflection of that love. When we heed God's warnings, we are able to avoid the consequences of disobedience and walk in His ways.

Disobedience Leads to Destruction

The people of Israel suffered greatly because they refused to listen to the warnings of the prophets. They experienced famine, war, and exile as a result of their disobedience. Similarly, when we refuse to listen to God's warnings, we open ourselves up to the destructive consequences of sin. Let us heed the warnings of the Lord and turn from our wicked ways.

Listen to the Voice of Truth

In a world full of competing voices, it can be difficult to discern the truth. But as followers of Christ, we have the Holy Spirit to guide us and the Word of God to instruct us. Let us turn to the Lord for guidance and wisdom, and let us be careful to listen to His voice above all others.

Let us take the warnings of God seriously and seek to obey Him with all our hearts. May we be discerning in all that we listen to, and may we turn to the Lord for guidance and wisdom. Let us walk in obedience and avoid the destructive consequences of disobedience.

Is there an area in your life that you are walking in disobedience or sin?

Who in your life can you trust to talk it out with?

Prayer:

Heavenly Father, we thank you for your love and your mercy. We thank you for the warnings that you give us through your Word and through the prompting of the Holy Spirit. Help us to be discerning in all that we listen to, and may we have ears to hear your voice above all others. Give us the strength to obey your commands and to avoid the destructive consequences of sin. We ask this in Jesus' name.

THE POWER OF DIVINE INTERVENTION

Ezra 6:14 (NLT) So the Jewish elders continued their work, and they were greatly encouraged by the preaching of the prophets Haggai and Zechariah son of Iddo. The Temple was finally finished, as had been commanded by the God of Israel and decreed by Cyrus, Darius, and Artaxerxes, the kings of Persia.

A friend I grew up with owned a company that was beginning to do really well. A larger company began to get very concerned at his success. It turns out, they did some shady things in order to try to damage my friends company. My friend decided to be honorable and not retaliate in anyway. After a while, things were discovered, his company was not only compensated financially but also word got out of how he handled things and his business surpassed the performance of the other company.

The book of Ezra tells the story of the return of the exiles from Babylon to Jerusalem, and their attempt to rebuild the temple that had been destroyed by the Babylonians. But their efforts faced significant obstacles, including opposition from the neighboring peoples, lack of resources, and the indifference of the Persian kings. Yet, through it all, God's hand was at work, orchestrating events and using unlikely allies to accomplish his purposes.

As the temple is finally completed and dedicated. But what is most remarkable about this story is the role played by King Darius of Persia. Despite the initial opposition from his officials, he eventually orders the construction to continue and even provides funding for the project. This is a stunning turn of events, as it was the Persians who had defeated the Babylonians and taken the Jews into exile.

What we see here is the power of divine intervention. Even when it seems like all hope is lost, God can use even our enemies to bring about his purposes. He can soften hearts, open doors, and provide resources in ways that we never thought possible. This is a reminder that we should never give up on our dreams or our callings, even when the obstacles seem insurmountable. We can trust that God is with us, working behind the scenes, and bringing about his plans in ways that we cannot imagine.

As we face the challenges and uncertainties of our own lives, let us remember the story of Ezra and the rebuilding of the temple. Let us trust in the power of divine intervention, and be open to the unexpected ways that God may choose to work in our lives. Let us be persistent in our efforts, but also humble and patient, knowing that God's timing is perfect and his ways are higher than our ways.

Do you remember a time where your integrity served you well?

Are you faced with a decision between living honorably or getting your way?

Prayer:

Dear God, we thank you for your faithfulness and your power to intervene in our lives. Help us to trust in your plans and to be open to the unexpected ways that you may choose to work. Give us courage to face the obstacles that come our way, and patience to wait for your perfect timing. We pray that you would use us to bring about your purposes in this world, and that we would be faithful to the callings that you have placed on our lives. Amen.

THE COST OF
FOLLOWING JESUS

Jeremiah 39:18 (NIV) - "I will rescue you on that day, declares the Lord; you will not be given into the hands of those you fear."

In 2017 the Lord sent me to Europe to minister where I would have the opportunity to put on a worship conference and speak at a few churches. A little ways before my trip, I was laid off from my job and basically ran out of money since it was very difficult to find a job that would let me work for a month and a half then take three weeks off then come back. I had 10 people who had committed one year prior, but all had backed out (for good reasons). I was sitting and asking myself should I still go. Then I got a notification on my phone that there was a terror attack in one of the countries I was planning to go to.

I knew I needed to go when I saw what had happened. I had completed a project that was supposed to pay me $1,000 when I arrived in LA on my way to Europe. The money did not come. This mean that I got on a plane to Europe with $72 to my name. I was terrified. I had never been away from Hawaii for this long at one time, and I was heading to one of the most expensive countries in the world.

I wanted to turn back so badly, people had canceled on me, I was leaving with no safety net. But I knew that God wanted me there, that was all I needed I returned home with more money than I left with.

Following Jesus is not always easy. The road may be long and winding, and it may come with great difficulties and even persecution. But as Christians, we must understand that there is a high cost to following Jesus, and we must be prepared to pay that cost.

In Jeremiah 39, we see Jeremiah being thrown into prison for speaking the word of God to the people of Israel. He was imprisoned for at least two and a half years, and it was not an easy time for him. But even in prison, Jeremiah never wavered in his faith. He continued to trust in God, knowing that He would rescue him.

As Christians, we are not promised a life free of pain, persecution, and trials. In fact, Jesus Himself told us that we will face difficulties in this life. However, we are promised that God will never leave us or forsake us, and that He will rescue us in our time of need.

When we choose to follow Jesus, we must be prepared to count the cost. We must be willing to endure trials and persecution for His sake. But we must also remember that God is faithful and that He will always be with us, no matter what we face.

In the end, the cost of following Jesus is worth it. For in Him, we have eternal life, and there is no greater reward than that.

Let us pray for the strength to follow Jesus, even when it is difficult. Let us ask God to help us count the cost and to be willing to pay it. And let us remember that no matter what we face in this life, God is always with us, and He will never leave us or forsake us.

There is always going to be a cost to following Jesus, The bible says that you should count the cost before you begin building. Have you counted the cost for yourself?

What will it look like if you were to go after it and trust that the Lord will provide all that you need?

Prayer

Dear God, we thank You for the gift of salvation and for the opportunity to follow Jesus. Help us to count the cost and to be willing to pay it. Give us the strength to endure trials and persecution for His sake. And help us to remember that You are always with us, no matter what we face. In Jesus' name, we pray. Amen.

TOO MUCH GOD NOT ENOUGH SPACE

1 Kings 8:11 (NLT) - "The priests could not continue their service because of the cloud, for the glorious presence of the Lord filled the Temple of the Lord."

One of the areas I have struggled with is trusting the Lord in the area of finances. I believe that is why the majority of the mission trips I have been on have had temporary or permanent layoffs leading up to the flight.

The first time I was invited to go on a mission trip, I told the mission team leader I would pray for a week. I knew when he asked that I was supposed to go but I was going to spend the week asking the Lord to change his mind. I told him the following week after church that I would go. I went to work on Monday like any normal Monday. When I got to work, my boss told me that if a check didn't arrive that day we would be taking the rest of the week off. At the end of the second week being laid off, I went off to see my grandmother. By the time I got home, I was yet again out of money.

The invitation was very last minute so I was I need of the trip fees within two weeks. I told the Lord, I think you want me to go, but now I can't pay for anything. I don't know how to fundraise but I am going to give it a shot. I typed out a letter and could only afford to print 50 copies, I handed out 8 at a leadership meeting for a ministry that I was a part of at the time. The following day, I was sitting in our church a few hours before our service when someone handed me an envelope. When I opened it, there was a check with the full amount of the mission trip fees. I felt like the room was closing in on me and I could barely breathe. I felt like God was so present that there was not enough room in the church for the both of us. I walked out of the building to get some air. It really reminded me of this scripture.

The Temple of the Lord was a magnificent structure, built to house the very presence of God. When the temple was completed, and the Ark of the Covenant was brought in, a cloud descended, filling the temple with the glorious presence of the Lord. The priests were unable to continue their service, overwhelmed by the holiness and power of God.

In our lives, we often try to fit God into a small space. We have our daily routines, our plans, and our priorities, and we try to squeeze God in somewhere in between. We give Him a few minutes of our time in the morning or before bed, or we attend church on Sundays, but we don't always make room for Him in our everyday lives.

But just like the priests in the temple, we can't contain the presence of God in a small space. When we invite Him into our lives, He wants to fill every area, every corner, and every moment. He wants to be the center of our lives, not an afterthought or a side note.

When we allow God to take up space in our lives, it can be overwhelming. We may feel like we can't continue with our usual routines or plans because His presence is so powerful. But that's exactly what we need. We need to be reminded that He is in control, that He is holy and powerful, and that He is worthy of our praise and worship.

So let's make room for God in our lives. Let's not try to fit Him into a small space or compartmentalize Him. Let's invite Him to take up space in every area of our lives, knowing that His presence will bring peace, joy, and fulfillment.

Spend some time reading a sitting quietly with God to understand the greatness of who God is.

Prayer

Dear God, we invite you to take up space in our lives. We acknowledge that we cannot contain your presence in a small space, and we ask that you fill every area of our lives. Help us to make room for you in our routines, our plans, and our priorities, knowing that your presence will bring peace, joy, and fulfillment. Thank you for your love and your grace. In Jesus' name, Amen.

REMEMBERED ACCORDING TO LOVE

Psalm 25:7 (NIV)

Do not remember the sins of my youth
and my rebellious ways;
according to your love remember me,
for you, Lord, are good.

Everyone has a past. You nor I are exempt from that fact, more than that, the bible is clear that past or not, we all miss the mark regarding sin. Mistakes I have made disqualify me for things, but God calls me redeemed. As humans, we have all made mistakes in our youth and rebelled against authority, but it is comforting to know that God doesn't define us by our past. Instead, He sees us through the lens of His love and mercy. He remembers us according to His love, not according to our mistakes.

God doesn't have the human ability to forget. His memory and everything else about Him is perfect. This means that the only way he can forget is if He chooses to do so. Also, something that I have heard said is that God loves us in spite of what we've done. The truth is that, God loves us, period. It's not in spite of anything, it is because He chooses to love us.

In Psalm 25:7, David is acknowledging his sinfulness and asking the Lord to not remember the sins of his youth and his rebellious ways. It is a beautiful reminder that God is a loving and forgiving God, who is willing to cast our sins as far as the east is from the west.

As humans, we have all made mistakes in our youth and rebelled against authority, but it is comforting to know that God doesn't define us by our past. Instead, He sees us through the lens of His love and mercy. He remembers us according to His love, not according to our mistakes.

When we come to God in repentance, we can rest assured that He forgives us completely and doesn't hold our past against us. He remembers us for who we are in Him, not who we were before we knew Him. Our past doesn't define us, and it doesn't limit God's love for us.

It is important to remember that we are all sinners and fall short of the glory of God, but when we come to Him with a repentant heart, He forgives us and forgets our past mistakes.

We are then able to move forward with the assurance that we are loved and accepted by Him.

Here is the paradox the more we focus on our shortcomings, the more we continue carry guilt which will keep us wanting to sin more to mask that guilt. Let go of the guilt so you can move forward.

God doesn't remember the sins of our youth, so stop spending so much time thinking about it.

Prayer:

Dear God, we thank you for your love and mercy that knows no bounds. We ask that you help us to remember that we are not defined by our past mistakes, but by your love for us. Help us to live our lives in a way that honors you, and to always turn to you with a repentant heart. We pray this in Jesus' name, Amen.

THE PAINFUL LOVE
OF GOD

Hosea 11:8 (NLT) "Oh, how can I give you up, Israel? How can I let you go? How can I destroy you like Admah or demolish you like Zeboiim? My heart is torn within me, and my compassion overflows.

I remember seeing the video of a very old military veteran speak about the change of the country that he fought for. The pain in the shaking of his voice as he spoke of the country that his brothers fought and died for. Whether you agree with his words or belief, you could feel his anguish in every word. The world he had fought for was falling apart in his eyes.

God created the world and then watched those he created destroy it, desecrate His name and do horrific things. The people He spoke to, called his chosen, decided that they didn't need him. In fact did everything they could to disrespect and disregard him.

My friend told me a story of when he brought home a bad report card to his father. He handed it to him and his father looked over it and smiled. His father took him out for dinner and dessert. He took him home and didn't say a word about the poor grades. My friend told me that the compassion that his father had for him affected him so deeply that he never got a bad grade again.

This is what the love of the Father should cause you to do.

In the book of Hosea, we see the story of a prophet who was instructed by God to marry a prostitute as a symbol of God's love for His unfaithful people. Hosea's life and message were a reflection of God's love and pain for the children of Israel. The passage in Hosea 8-11 talks about the judgment of the Lord on the children of Israel and the love that the Lord has for His children.

As we read through these chapters, we see the painful love of God for His people. In Hosea 11:8, we see a God who loves so much that He would speak words like "Oh, how can I give you up, Israel?" The Lord's heart is torn within Him because of His love for His people. Even though the children of Israel have been unfaithful to Him, God's love is still steadfast and unfailing.

But why don't we see this love in our day to day lives? Why don't we trust Him and follow Him if He is that loving and trustworthy? Perhaps it is because we get caught up in our own ways and desires. We forget that God's love is all-encompassing, and He wants what is best for us. We must learn to trust Him even when we cannot see the road ahead.

God's love is not just a feeling, but it is an action. In Hosea 11:4, God says, "I led them with cords of human kindness, with ties of love. To them, I was like one who lifts a little child to the cheek and I bent down to feed them." The Lord's love for us is tangible and real, and it is something we can experience in our lives.

The love of God drove Him to send His Son to die for our sins. Let us not take for granted the love that God has for us. Let us trust Him and follow Him, knowing that He has our best interests at heart.

With the full understanding of the love of the Father, How can you live your life to honor Him?

Prayer:
Dear God, thank You for loving us even when we are unfaithful to You. Help us to trust You and follow You with all our hearts. May Your love be tangible in our lives, and may we never forget the pain and sacrifice that went into it. In Jesus' name, we pray. Amen.

Thank you for taking the time to go through this devotional, I pray that you have found some hope and healing throughout these last 40 days.

Made in the USA
Las Vegas, NV
30 May 2023

72744802R00079